101 Fun Crossword Puzzles
for Clever Kids

This book belongs to:

_____

Thank you for choosing our crossword puzzle book. It's so cool that you like crosswords as much as we do! Crosswords offer hours of entertainment, and they're a great way to relax while learning problem solving, spelling, and vocabulary.

Crossword puzzles are like a mystery game made out of words. Each page has an empty grid and a list of clues to help you figure out which words to fill into the grid. It sounds easy, but some of the clues are pretty tricky!

We start off easy with small grids and fewer clues so you can get comfortable solving crosswords. As you progress through the book, the crosswords will get harder! You'll have to solve more clues to fill in bigger grids. This helps you to get more confident in your abilities every time you solve a puzzle.

We recommend using a pencil. Write in your guess for each clue as you go; if it doesn't fit, or if a word it crosses over with different letters, you will be able to erase it. The solution to every crossword puzzle is at the top of each page.

Our large puzzles are easy to see, and we've included cute pictures to make them more fun for you to solve.

Have fun and happy puzzling!

Jennifer L. Trace

Level 1

Let's get started!

In this level, you'll have to solve 3 or 4 clues to fill in the puzzle.

How to Get Around

INSTRUCTIONS: Put words to the pictures to solve the puzzle.

At the Park

GRASS   TREE   SLIDE

INSTRUCTIONS: Put words to the pictures to solve the puzzle.

Ocean Creatures

FISH   WHALE   SEAL

INSTRUCTIONS: Put words to the pictures to solve the puzzle.

Fresh Fruit

PEAR   PEACH   APPLE

INSTRUCTIONS: Put words to the pictures to solve the puzzle.

At the Zoo

LION   BEAR   TIGER

INSTRUCTIONS: Put words to the pictures to solve the puzzle.

Green Giants

TRUNK   TREE   LEAF

INSTRUCTIONS: Put words to the pictures to solve the puzzle. You may notice some numbers with a letter next to them such as '2D or 2A'. D stands for Down and A stands for Across.

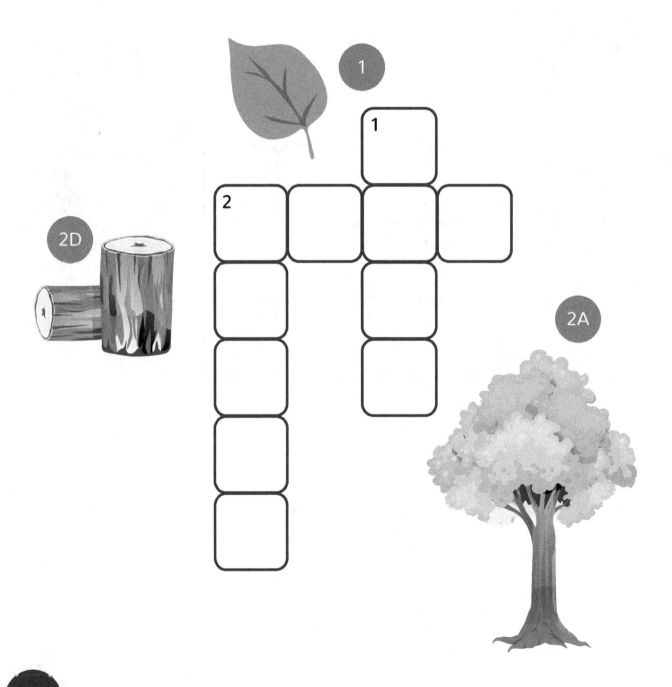

On the Farm

COW   EGG   HORSE

INSTRUCTIONS: Put words to the pictures to solve the puzzle.

In Full Bloom

FLOWER   STEM   LEAF

INSTRUCTIONS: Put words to the pictures to solve the puzzle.

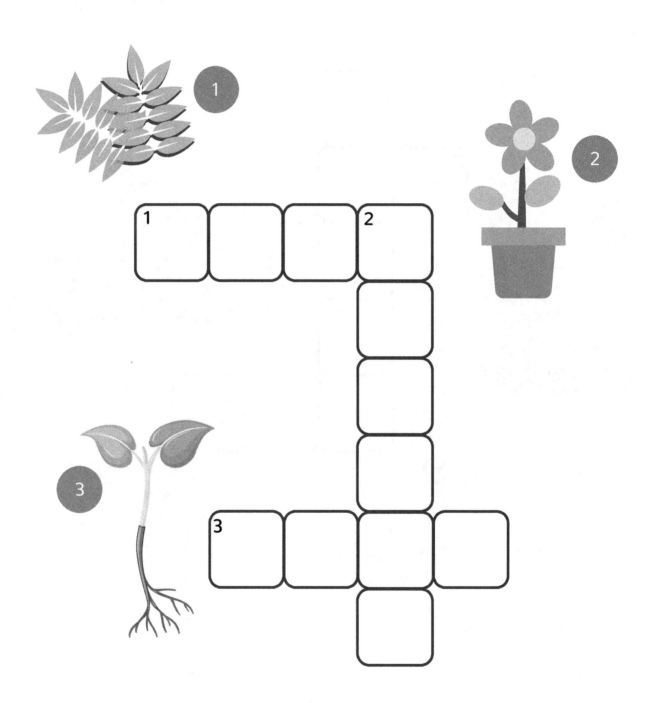

A Quick Checkup

NURSE   DOCTOR   BED

NSTRUCTIONS: Put words to the pictures to solve the puzzle.

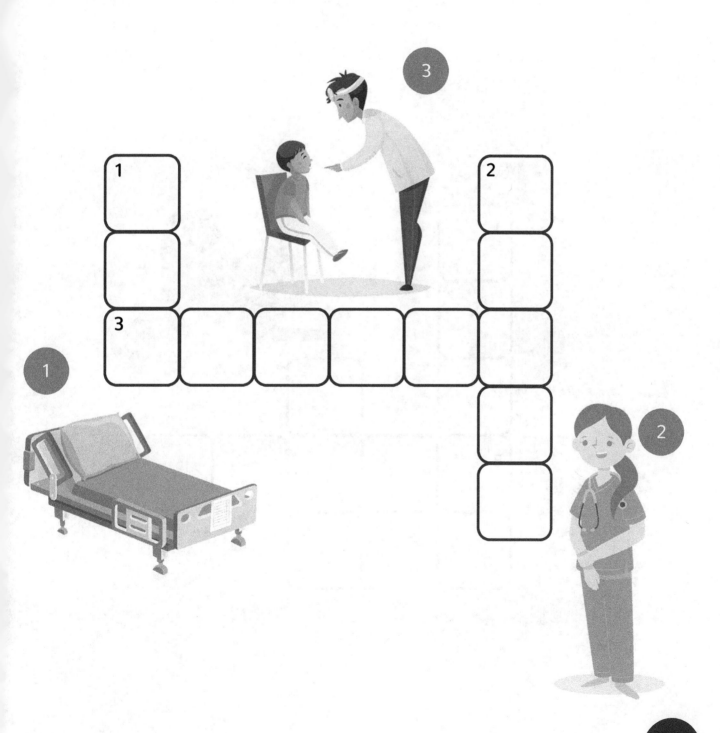

Different People, Different Pets

MOUSE   CAT   SNAKE

INSTRUCTIONS: Put words to the pictures to solve the puzzle.

Long 'O' Sounds

MOW   TOW   BOAT

INSTRUCTIONS: Solve the clues to fill in the puzzle.

Across

2. As a chore, you might __ the lawn.
3. A __-truck pulls other cars.

Down

1. A __ is a ship that floats on water.

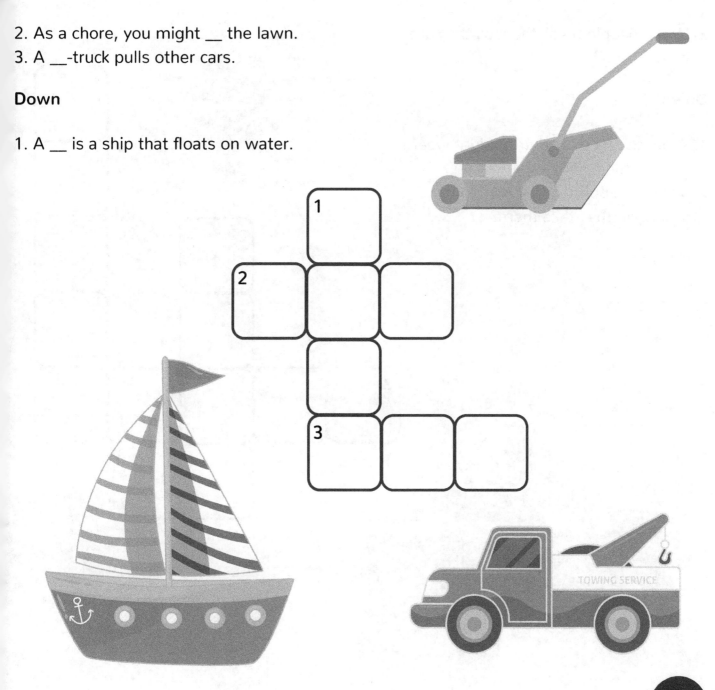

Police Station

JAIL   CRIME   BADGE

INSTRUCTIONS: Solve the clues to fill in the puzzle.

Across

3. When people break the law, they are committing a __.

Down

1. A police officer or sheriff might wear a __ on their shirt.
2. When the police arrest someone, where do they take them?

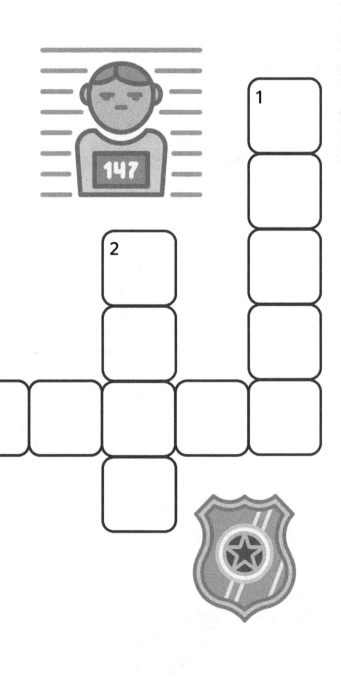

Counting Up

TEN   FOUR   TWO

INSTRUCTIONS: Solve the clues to fill in the puzzle.

Across

1. How many toes do most people have on their feet?
2. How many legs do most dogs and cats have?

Down

1. How many eyes do most people have on their face?

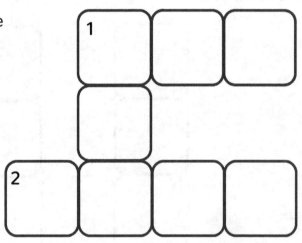

Time for Bed

DREAM   SLEEP   BED

INSTRUCTIONS: Solve the clues to fill in the puzzle.

Across

3. You might have a sweet __ at
   night instead of a nightmare.

Down

1. Where you lie down at bedtime.
2. When it's time for bed, you
   go to __.

Size Words

TINY   BIG   LITTLE

INSTRUCTIONS: Solve the clues to fill in the puzzle.

Across

2. Something large, like a __ mountain or elephant.
3. Something really really small is __.

Down

1. Something small, like a __ mouse or kitten.

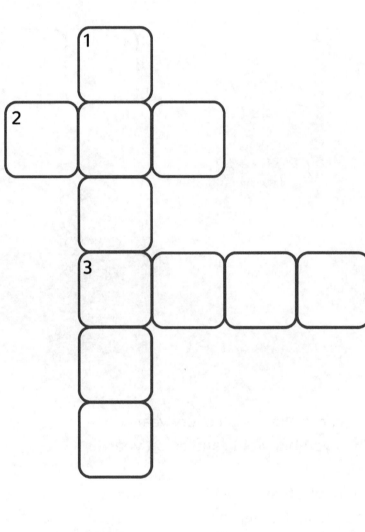

17

Make a Wish!

INSTRUCTIONS: Solve the clues to fill in the puzzle.

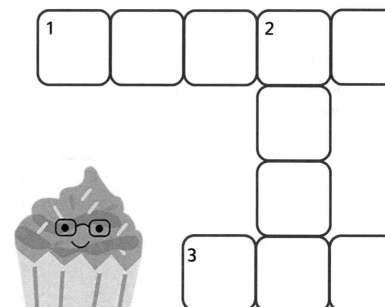

Across

1. You can make a wish every year when you blow out candles on your __day.
3. You might toss a coin in this watery place, called a wishing __.

Down

2. When you make a wish, you hope it will come __.
4. Some people will blow on a dande__ and make a wish.

Tide Pooling

SHELL   CRAB   SEA   WEED

NSTRUCTIONS: Solve the clues to fill in the puzzle.

Across

2. Sea creatures like clams live inside these, but you can collect empty ones on the beach.
3. A hermit __ is a small animal that lives inside a shell.

Down

1. Most of the plants that wash up on the beach are sea__.
2. The ocean is also called the __.

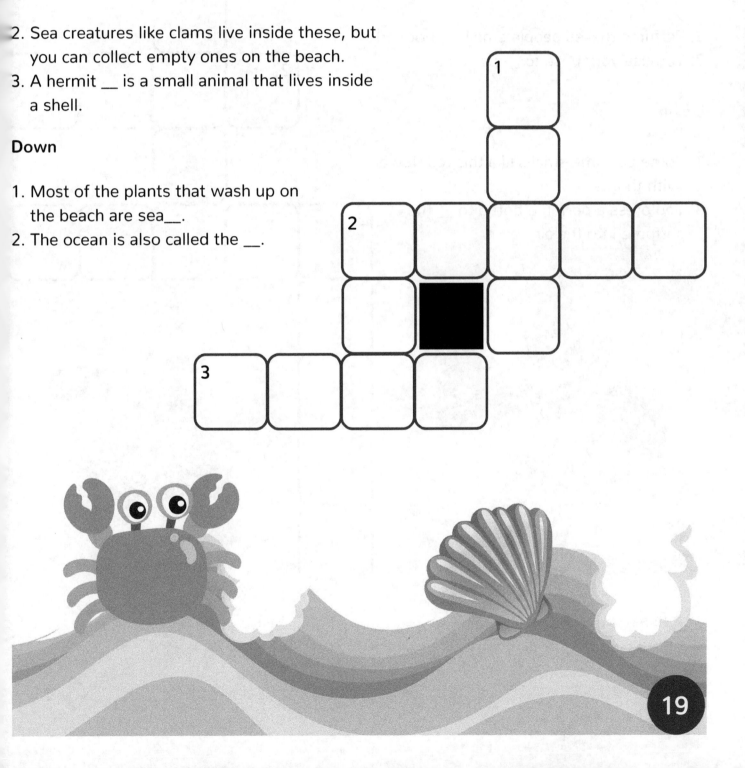

Perfume Shop

SPRAY   SMELL   ROSE   GOOD

INSTRUCTIONS: Solve the clues to fill in the puzzle.

Across

2. Perfume makes people smell __, not bad.
3. You use your nose to __ perfume.

Down

1. Some perfume smells like this red flower with thorns.
3. You press a perfume bottle to __ the perfume into the air.

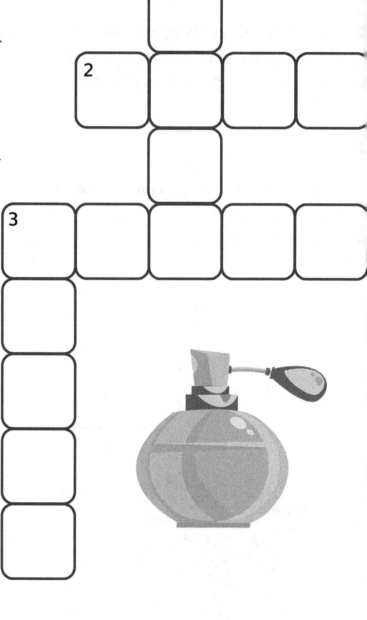

Fast Food

DRINK   FRY   CHICKEN   HAM

INSTRUCTIONS: Solve the clues to fill in the puzzle.

Across

2. Lots of people order __burgers at fast food restaurants.
4. You can get water, juice, or a soda to __ while you eat your food.

Down

1. Some people order __ nuggets to eat.
3. A french __ is a good thing to eat with a burger.

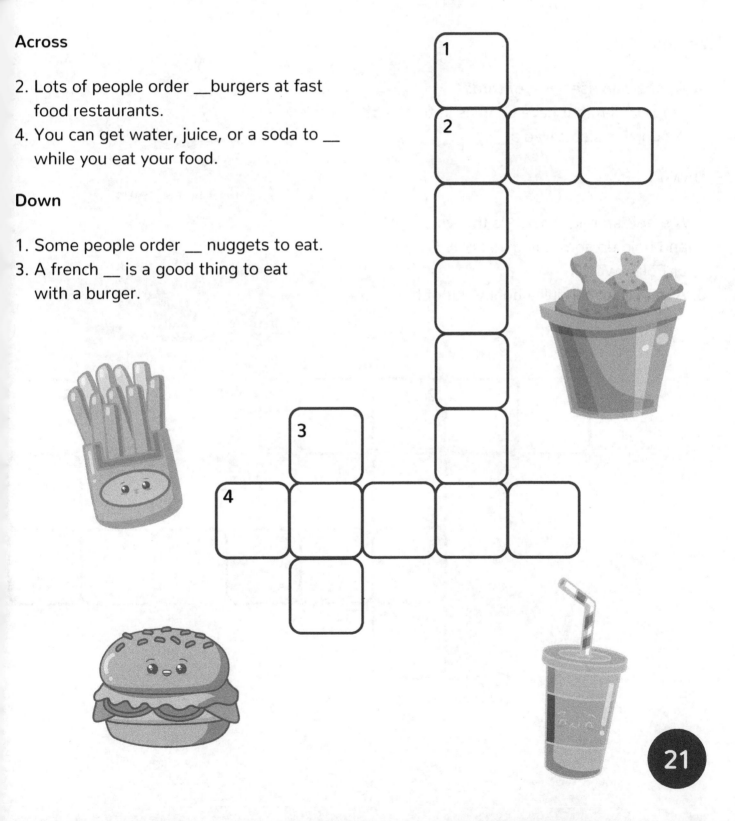

Magic Trick

RABBIT   HAT   DECK   CARD

INSTRUCTIONS: Solve the clues to fill in the puzzle.

Across

1. A magician uses a __ of cards.
4. Magicians might have bunnies in their act!
   A bunny is also called a __.

Down

2. A magician might ask: "Is this your __?",
   and hold up something you play Go Fish
   or Poker with.
3. A magician will pull a bunny out of her __.

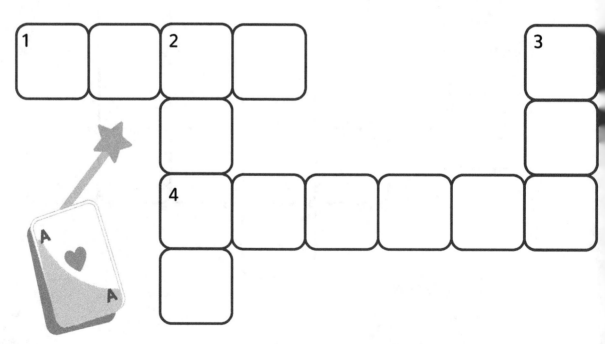

Royal Family

QUEEN   RULE   KING   PRINCE

INSTRUCTIONS: Solve the clues to fill in the puzzle.

Across

2. A man who runs a kingdom or is married to a queen.
4. A king or a queen will __ over a kingdom.

Down

1. The son of a king or a queen.
3. A woman who runs a kingdom or is married to a king.

Creepy Crawlies

FLY   BEE   LICE   BUG

INSTRUCTIONS: Solve the clues to fill in the puzzle.

Across

1. An insect can also be called a __.
3. Be careful not to get little itchy bugs called __ in your hair.

Down

1. This insect has black and yellow stripes and a stinger.
2. This insect is black, has wings, and makes a buzzing sound.

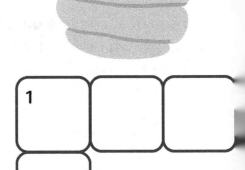

My Face

EARS   EYES   NOSE   LIPS

INSTRUCTIONS: Solve the clues to fill in the puzzle.

Across

2. I have two __ that I use to see.
3. I have one __ that I use to smell.

Down

1. My mouth has two __ that can smile.
2. I have two __ I use to hear.

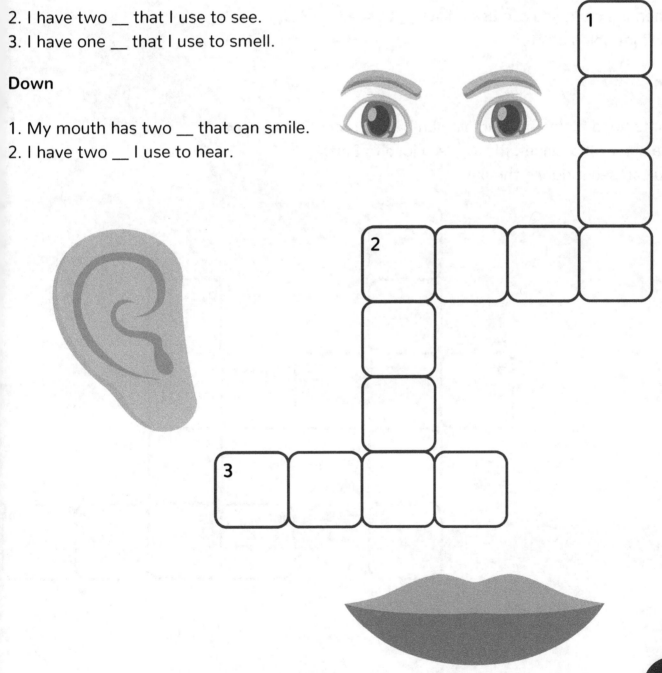

Here Comes The Sun

LIGHT   STAR   SHINE   GROW

INSTRUCTIONS: Fill in the blanks to solve the puzzle.

Across

3. When it's dark, you can use a flash__ to see.
4. Sunlight helps plants __.

Down

1. Plants need plenty of light, air, sun__ and water.
2. The sun isn't a planet, it's a __ so close to Earth you can see it during the day.

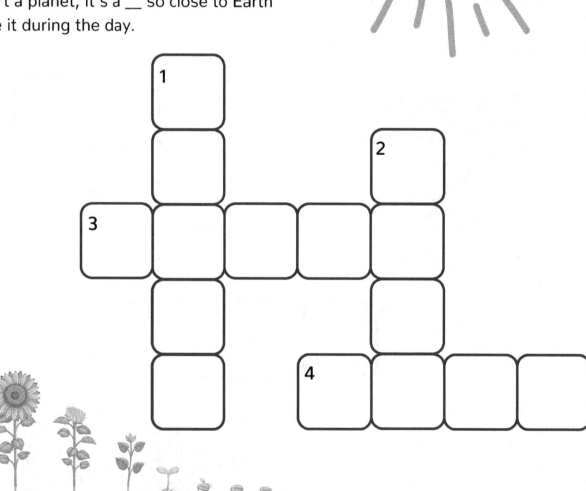

Living Room

CARPET   TABLE   LAMP   CHAIR

INSTRUCTIONS: Solve the clues to fill in the puzzle.

Across

2. A piece of furniture you sit in, sometimes made of wood.
3. A big piece of furniture you put things on, like a dining room ___.

Down

1. A small piece of furniture that lights up.
2. A soft rug you spread across the floor.

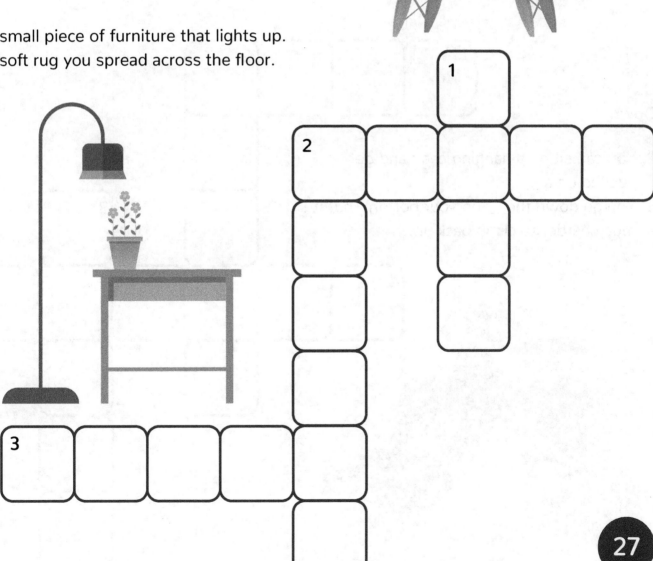

The Playground

SWING   BARS   SLIDE   JUNGLE

INSTRUCTIONS: Solve the clues to fill in the puzzle.

Across

1. You can swing around on the monkey __.
4. Some kids call their playground a __ gym, it's also the forested place where monkeys and jaguars live.

Down

2. You can sit on a hanging chair and get pushed on a __.
3. You go down the __ on your bottom, but it's much harder to climb back up.

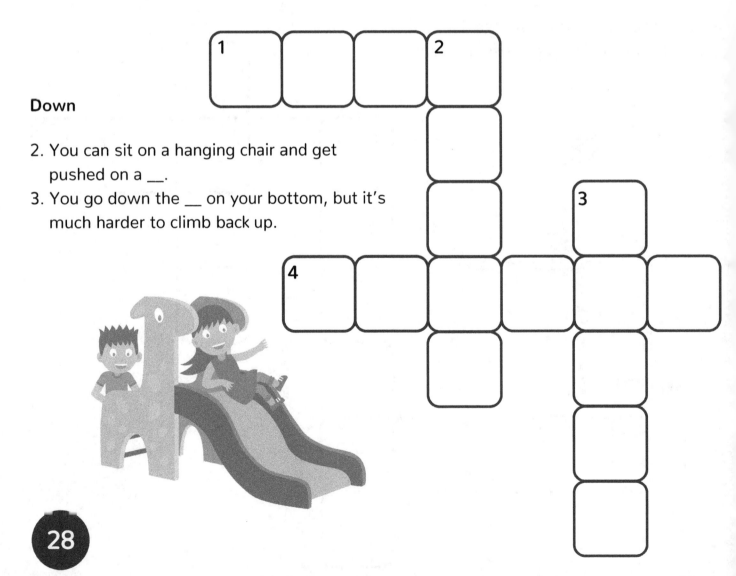

Dinner Time

BREAD   MILK   STEAK   CHICKEN

INSTRUCTIONS: Solve the clues to fill in the puzzle.

Across

3. A bird that lives on a farm.
4. A piece of meat that comes from a cow.

Down

1. Made out of flour, this soft and doughy baked good is served as a side.
2. You might have this drink that comes from a cow's udders.

Learn to Write

INSTRUCTIONS: Solve the clues to fill in the puzzle.

Across

2. When you write a new word, be sure to __ it right, putting all the right letters in the right order.
4. Be careful if you write with this; it contains ink that can't be erased.

Down

1. This yellow stick is a good tool to write with; you can erase it if you make a mistake.
3. You write on this flat sheet, made from trees and usually blank or white.

Sick Day

REST   COLD   SICK   FEVER

INSTRUCTIONS: Solve the clues to fill in the puzzle.

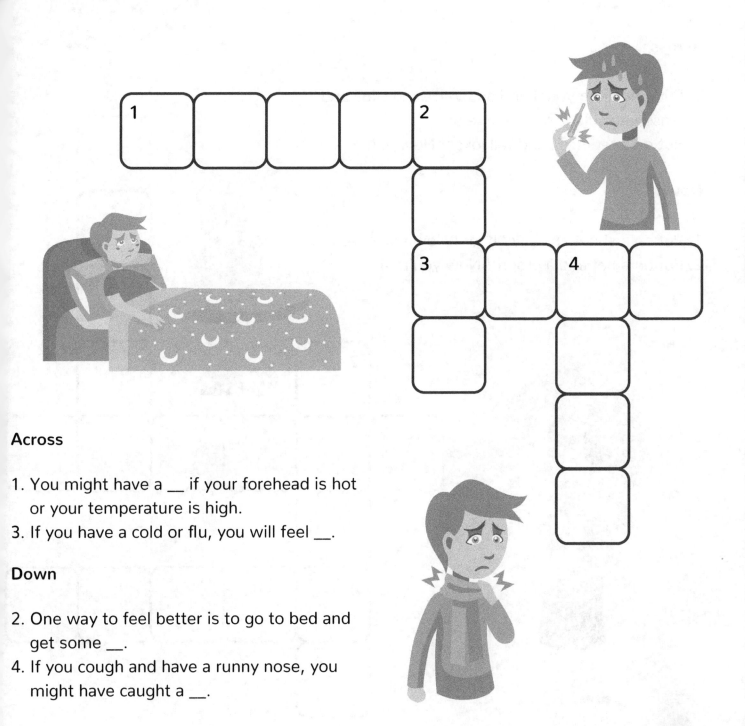

Across

1. You might have a __ if your forehead is hot or your temperature is high.
3. If you have a cold or flu, you will feel __.

Down

2. One way to feel better is to go to bed and get some __.
4. If you cough and have a runny nose, you might have caught a __.

Let's Play Dress-Up

PIRATE   CLOWN   GHOST   WITCH

INSTRUCTIONS: Name each costume to fill in the puzzle.

Across

3. Put a hook on your hand and wave the skull and crossbones flag! Now you're a:
4. Put on a red nose and tell jokes! Now you're a:

Down

1. Put on a sheet and say "boo"! Now you're a:
2. Put on a hat and a broom! Now you're a:

It's Valentine's Day!

CANDY   CARD   HEART   LOVE

INSTRUCTIONS: Solve the clues to fill in the puzzle.

Across

2. You might tell your friends and family: "I __ you!" on Valentine's Day.
3. A piece of paper with a message on it.

Down

1. You have one of these inside your body, and it's also the shape of cards and candies for Valentine's Day.
3. Sweet treats you can give as gifts.

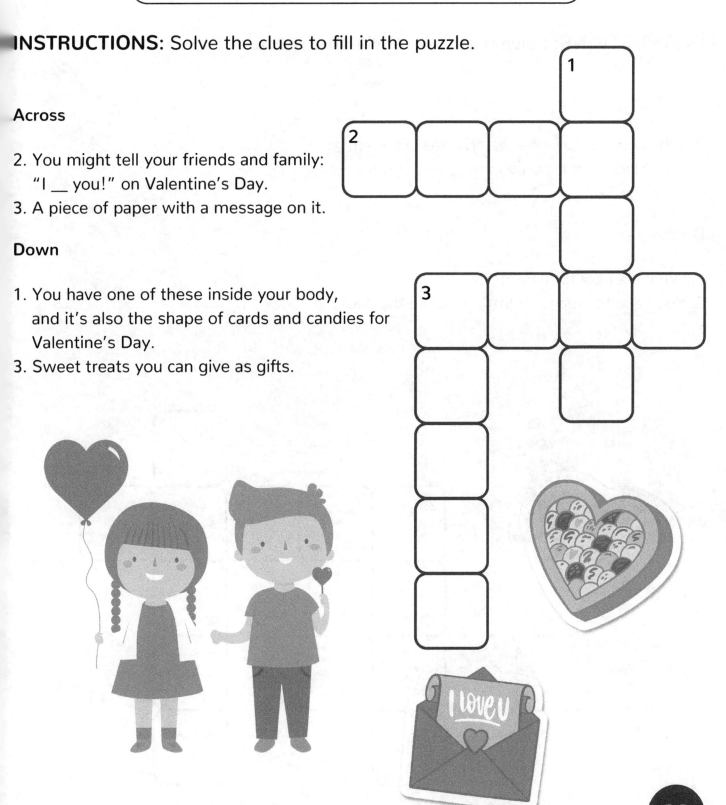

A Trip to the Pool

SPLASH   SWIM   WATER   SUIT

INSTRUCTIONS: Solve the clues to fill in the puzzle.

Across

2. When you jump in the water, it makes a big __.
3. If you kick your legs, you can __ through the water like a fish.

Down

1. What's a pool filled with?
2. You have to wear a swim__ to get in the pool.

At the Movie Theatre

TOON   POP   SCREEN   SCARY

INSTRUCTIONS: Fill in the blanks to solve the puzzle.

Across

1. Horror movies can be really __.
3. A drawn or animated movie can be
   called a car__.

Down

1. The movie plays on a big __.
2. You might eat __corn when you watch
   a movie.

The Museum Gallery

PAINT   ART   PHOTO   FRAME

INSTRUCTIONS: Fill in the blanks to solve the puzzle.

Across

1. A piece of art can be displayed inside a wooden border, called a picture __.
3. When a photographer takes a picture with a camera, the picture is called a __graph.

Down

2. Paintings, drawings, statues, and photographs are all pieces of __.
3. Artists put many kinds of colorful __ on a canvas to make a painting.

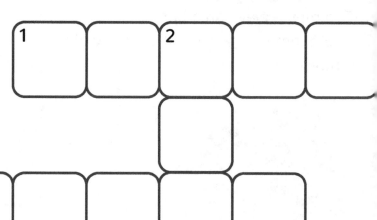

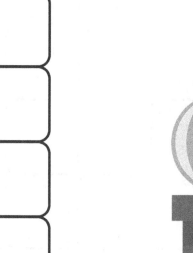

Play Piano

BLACK   WHITE   MUSIC   FINGERS

INSTRUCTIONS: Solve the clues to fill in the puzzle.

Across

2. Some piano keys are __, the color of snow.
4. You can make __ when you play a song on any instrument.

Down

1. You play the piano using the ten __ on both of your hands.
3. Some piano keys are __, the color of the night sky.

Level 2

Nice work!

Now that you've had some practice, you'll need to solve 5 or 6 clues to get through each of these crosswords.

Toy Chest

BALL   DOLL   CAR   BLOCK   DICE

INSTRUCTIONS: Figure out what toy you use for each kind of play

Across

1. These toys are square and have six sides with numbers or dots on them. Roll them to see what number you get!
2. This toy is shaped like a circle and might be bouncy.
3. This toy is a little version of something your parents might drive around in.

Down

1. This toy is shaped just like a little person.
2. You can build things out of this toy or stack a lot of them into a tower.

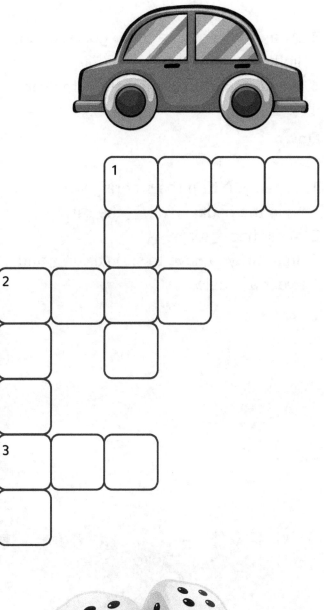

A Trip in the Car

SEAT   DRIVE   BELT   STOP   FOUR

INSTRUCTIONS: Solve the clues to fill in the puzzle.

Across

3. At a green light, cars can go. At a red light, cars have to __.
4. Wear a seat__ to stay safe in the car.

Down

1. When you turn the steering wheel and use the pedals, you __ the car.
2. A car has __ tires.
3. In a car, you have to sit in a car__ and wear a __belt.

It's Raining, It's Pouring

HAIL   COAT   MUD   DROP   PUDDLE

INSTRUCTIONS: Fill in the blanks to solve the puzzle.

Across

2. Each little bit of falling rain is called a rain__.
5. If rain freezes into ice as it falls, it makes __.

Down

1. When dirt gets wet, it becomes __.
3. With rain boots on, you can jump in a __ without getting wet!
4. Wear a rain __ to stay dry in a storm.

Open the Closet

DRESS   SHIRT   PANTS   SHOES   SKIRT

INSTRUCTIONS: What clothes should you wear?

Across

2. You wear a pair of these on your feet.
4. This piece of clothing is like a shirt and a skirt put together.

Down

1. You wear a pair of these on your legs.
2. Instead of pants, you can wear this to cover your legs. It's like the bottom half of a dress!
3. This piece of clothing has sleeves that can be long or short.

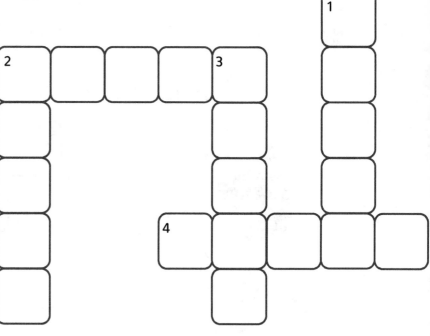

My House

FLOOR   DOOR   YARD   ROOF   STAIRS

INSTRUCTIONS: Solve the clues to fill in the puzzle.

Across

4. When you step inside, this is under your feet. It's also what you call other levels of your house, like the second __.

5. You might have a space around your house to play outside called a front or back __.

Down

1. These lead up or down, and take people to the first, second, or third floor of a house.
2. Something on top of the house. Could be said as "A ___ over your head".
3. This opens and closes to let people into your house and into different rooms.

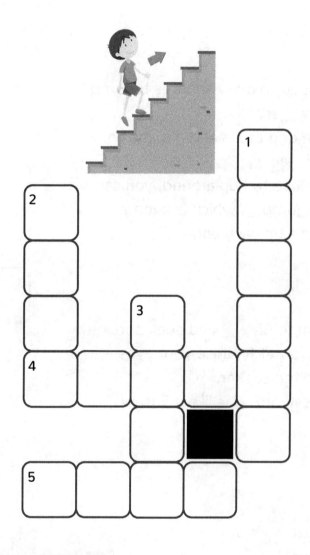

Game Time

PUZZLE   ROPE   TOE   HOP   HIDE

INSTRUCTIONS: Fill in the blanks to solve the puzzle!

Across

1. You need to draw squares to jump in to play __scotch.
3. With a grid of x's and o's, it's easy to play tic tac __.
4. If you love to hop around, you can play with a jump__, which is a long toy with a handle on each end.

Down

1. It's fun to play __ and seek outside! Don't forget to close your eyes if you're the seeker.
2. A crossword __ is like a jigsaw __.

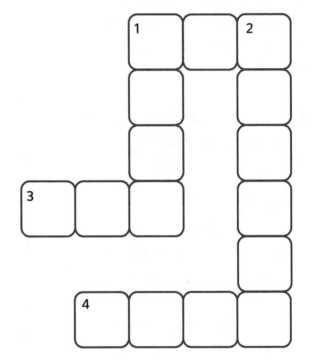

Set the Table

PLATE   SPOON   KNIFE   FORK   BOWL

INSTRUCTIONS: Solve the clues to fill in the puzzle.

Across

1. A utensil with three points that makes half a "spork".
4. A flat, usually round dish for putting solid food on.
5. A deep dish for putting soup, cereal, and other liquid food in.

Down

2. A utensil with a blade for cutting things.
3. A utensil with a rounded bowl on one end to scoop things up with.

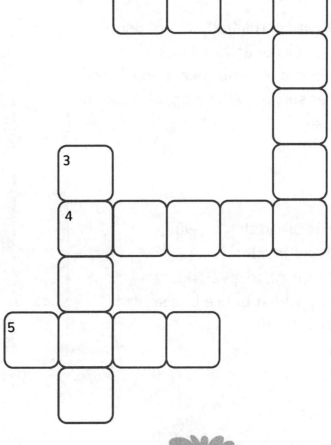

45

Time for Breakfast

PAN   BACON   TOAST   ORANGE   CEREAL

INSTRUCTIONS: Solve the clues to fill in the puzzle.

Across

4. Made with citrus fruit, lots of people drink __ juice with breakfast.
5. A flapjack is a round cake made from a batter served with syrup, also called a __cake.

Down

1. Crunchy bread that's been sliced and toasted.
2. Thin strips of crispy pork.
3. Crunchy wheat or rice bits served with milk.

It's Electric

PHONE   PUTER   VISION   LIGHT   TOP

INSTRUCTIONS: Complete the words to fill in the puzzle.

Across

2. A small personal computer is a lap__.
4. TV is short for tele__.
5. You can use the internet on a com__.

Down

1. __bulbs illuminate your whole house.
3. You can call people with a cell__.

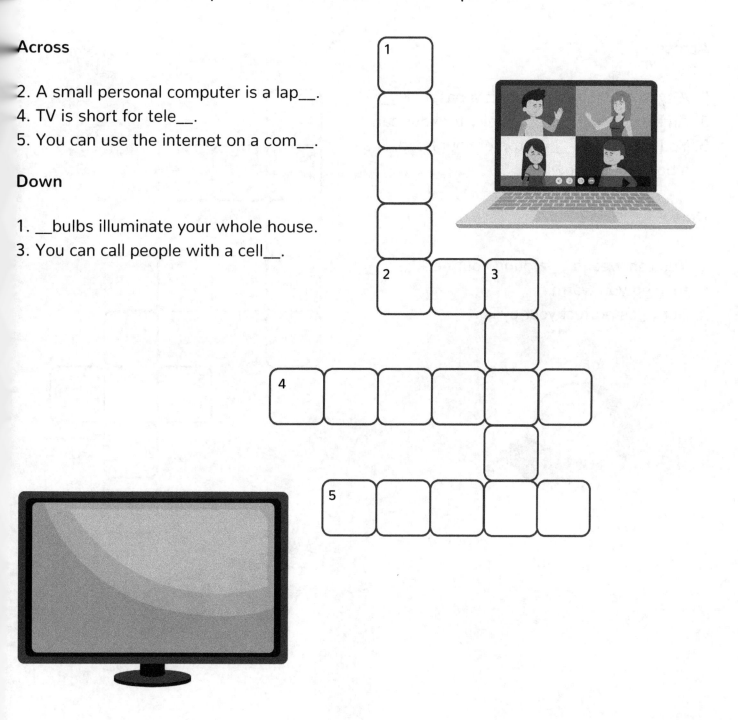

Around My Head

RING   GLASS   CAP   HAT   SCARF

INSTRUCTIONS: Solve the clues to fill in the puzzle.

Across

2. A type of hat with a brim is a baseball __.
3. An ear__ is a piece of jewelry for your ear.
5. You can wear a __ on top of your head, like a bonnet or a bowler.

Down

1. You can wear a __ around your neck to keep you warm.
4. Sun __es protect your eyes.

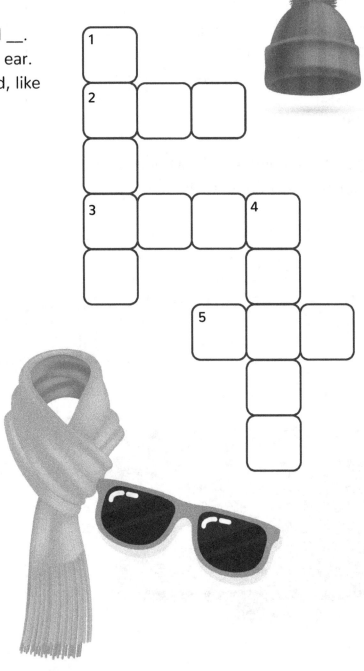

At the Faire

ROLLER   ROUND   HOUSE   RIDE   COTTON

INSTRUCTIONS: Solve the clues to fill in the puzzle.

Across

3. The carousel of ponies is also called a merry-go-__.
4. You can go down a big drop on the __ coaster.

Down

1. __ candy is pink, fluffy, and sweet.
2. You might get scared if you visit the haunted __!
4. Some signs will say: "You must be this tall to __".

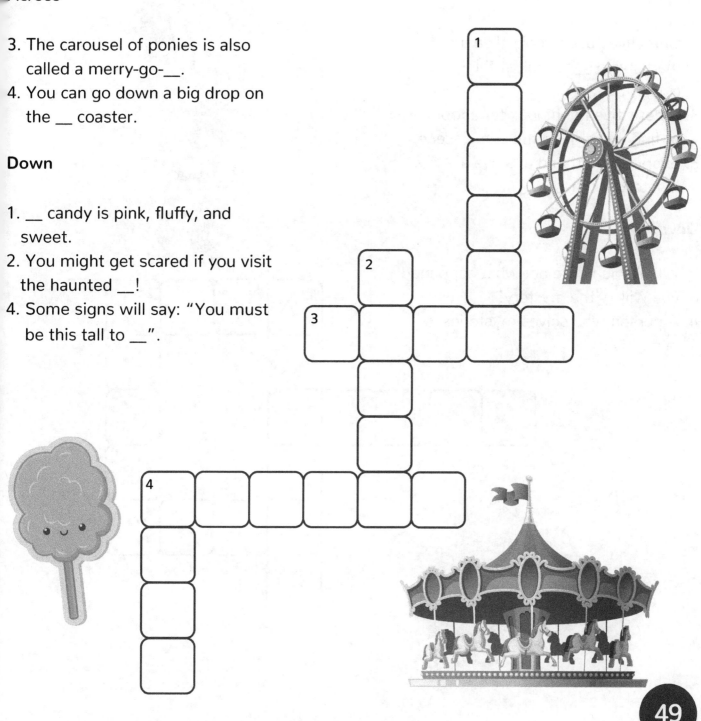

Let's Be a Detective

PRINT   TECT   CLUE   GLASS   SOLVE

INSTRUCTIONS: Solve the clues to fill in the puzzle.

Across

1. Detectives use a tool called a
   magnifying __ to look at things
   closely.
3. A detective might look for a foot
   or finger__ around the crime scene.
5. Every hint you find to solve a
   mystery is called a __.

Down

2. When you figure out what happened,
   you will __ the mystery!
4. A person who solves mysteries is
   a de__ive.

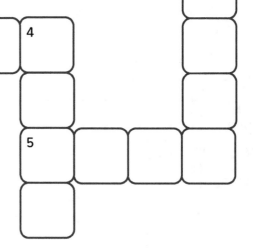

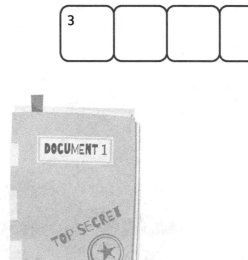

DOCUMENT 1

TOP SECRET

50

A Day at the Beach

SAIL   SAND   CASTLE   TOWEL   WAVE

NSTRUCTIONS: Solve the clues to fill in the puzzle.

Across

2. The beach is made up of many tiny grains of __.
4. You might see small boats called __ boats; they have masts and __s.
5. When you go to the beach, bring a blanket called a __ to dry off with or lie down on.

Down

1. You can shape sand into a big sand__ for a queen to live in.
3. A peak of water on the ocean is called a __, and they get bigger closer to shore.

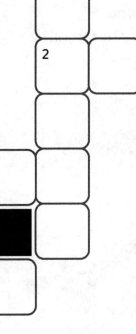

Firefighting Heroes

HOSE   STATION   TRUCK   FIRE   SMOKE

INSTRUCTIONS: Solve the clues to fill in the puzzle.

Across

2. You can spot a fire from far away by seeing black __ rising up.
4. Firefighters use a big __ to spray water on a fire.

Down

1. A firefighter might drive around in a big red fire__.
2. A building where firefighters stay at is called the firefighter __.
3. Firefighters will try to put out a house that is on __.

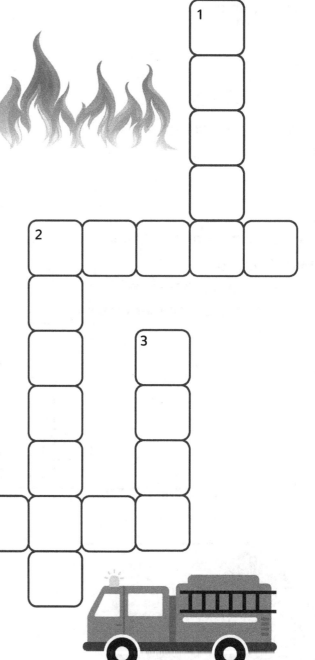

Baby Animals

CHICK   CUB   DUCK   LAMB   CALF

INSTRUCTIONS: Solve the clues to fill in the puzzle.

Across

2. A baby cow.
3. A baby bear, wolf, or lion.
4. A baby duck is called a __ling.

Down

1. A baby sheep.
3. A baby chicken.

My Body

ARMS   HANDS   TOES   HEAD   FEET

INSTRUCTIONS: Fill in the blanks to solve the puzzle.

Across

3. You have ten __ on your feet.
4. Your fingers are connected to your __.

Down

1. At the end of your legs, you have two __.
2. Your __ is on top of your neck.
5. You have two __ attached to your shoulders, with hands at the ends.

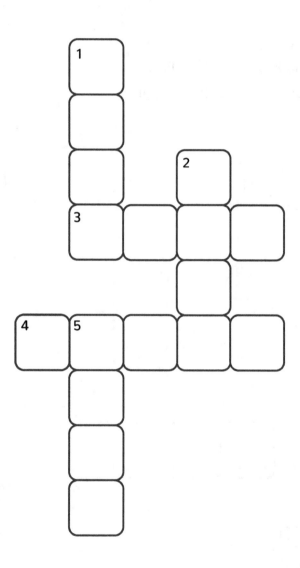

Movement Verbs

WALK   LIE   RUN   THROW   DANCE

NSTRUCTIONS: Solve the clues to fill in the puzzle.

Across

2. You can __ a ball or a frisbee.
5. Your dog might sit, __ down,
   and roll over.

Down

1. You can __ around to music.
3. You can __ fast around a track.
4. You can __ on the sidewalk.

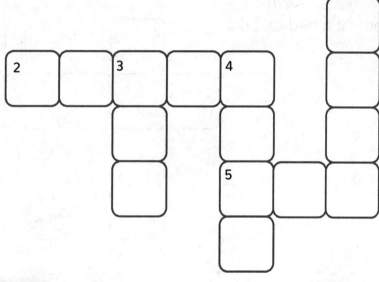

Now It's Autumn

INSTRUCTIONS: Solve the clues to fill in the puzzle.

Across

3. An autumn holiday called __giving where everyone eats turkey.
4. Farmers put __crows dressed as people in their fields.

Down

1. The leaves change __ from green to red.
2. Another word for the season of Autumn is __, because the leaves __ down.
3. At Thanksgiving, you eat a bird called a __.

A Day at School

NSTRUCTIONS: Solve the clues to fill in the puzzle.

Across

3. The person who teaches you at school is called a __.
4. When you go to school, you go to your __room with your other __mates.

Down

1. If you go to school, you are a __.
2. Every year, you move up a __, like when you go from first __ to second __.
3. When you take a quiz and answer questions, it might be called a __.

In the Sky

BLUE   BIRD   PLANE   STARS   SKY

INSTRUCTIONS: Solve the clues to fill in the puzzle.

Across

1. When you're outside and you look up, you can see the __.
2. An animal with wings is called a __.
3. In an air__, you can fly through the sky.

Down

1. At night, you can see the moon and __ shining. They form constellations.
2. During a clear day, the sky is __.

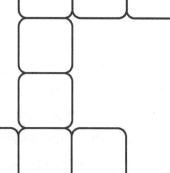

In the Car

SEAT   DRIVE   ROAD   WHEEL   TIRE   STOP

NSTRUCTIONS: Solve the clues to fill in the puzzle.

Across

2. A red sign with eight sides is a __ sign, telling cars to hit the brakes.
5. You can __ from place to place in a car.

Down

1. Cars drive on the __.
2. Remember to buckle your __belt.
3. Spin the steering __ to turn the car.
4. The car rides on four rubber wheels, each one is called a __. Don't get a flat __!

59

My Cat

MICE   MEOW   TAIL   CLAWS   WHISKER   PURR

INSTRUCTIONS: Solve the clues to fill in the puzzle.

Across

2. Inside their paws, a cat has sharp __.
5. Cats will chase small animals like rats and __.
6. A happy cat will __ if you pet it.

Down

1. Most cats have a long __ like a dog.
3. Cats have long thin hairs on their face, each one is called a __.
4. Cats make this sound:

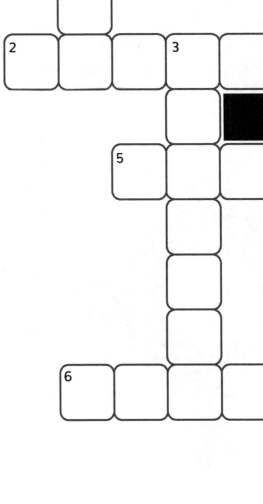

At the Library

AUTHOR PAGE CHAPTER READ WORD TITLE

NSTRUCTIONS: Solve the clues to fill in the puzzle.

Across

2. Every piece of paper in a book is called a:
3. A book has a name, called the __.
4. You can __ a book yourself or have someone else __ it out loud to you.
6. When you put letters together, it is called a __.

Down

1. Longer books have pieces called __s that go in order. You read __ one, then __ two...
5. The person who wrote a book.

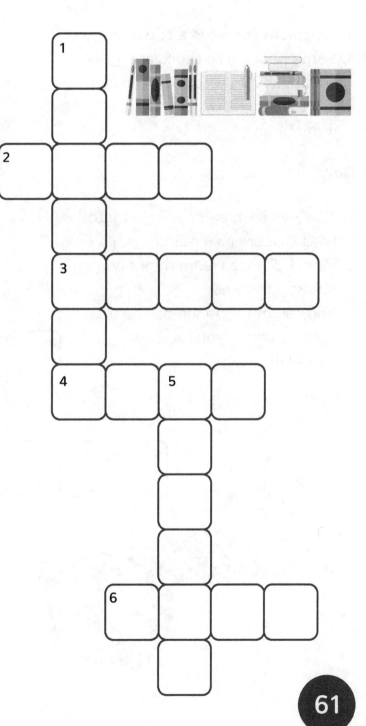

Ice Cream Parlor

CHIP   MINT   HOT   CONE   SCOOP   BERRY

INSTRUCTIONS: Solve the clues to fill in the puzzle.

Across

3. Ice cream comes in a cup or a __.
4. Some people like chocolate __ ice cream, like a chocolate __ cookie.
6. If ice cream tastes like a candy cane, it might be __.

Down

1. To serve ice cream, you __ it into balls that are also called __s. I'll take
2. Pink, fruity ice cream might be straw__ flavored.
5. You can get __ fudge on top of your sundae if you like your chocolate warm.

Now It's Christmas!

TREE   PRESENT   DEER   EVE   PLACE   SANTA

NSTRUCTIONS: Solve the clues to fill in the puzzle.

Across

1. Under the tree, you might find a gift, also called a __.
5. The night before Christmas is called Christmas __.

Down

1. A chimney is attached to the fire__.
2. __ Claus brings presents to some houses on Christmas.
3. You can decorate a pine __ with lights for Christmas.
4. The magic sleigh is pulled by rein__ like Rudolph.

63

The Farmer's Market

POTATO BEAN PEAS CARROT TOMATO BEET

INSTRUCTIONS: Solve the clues to fill in the puzzle.

Across

2. This small vegetable has lots of types, like string, black, pinto, kidney, and fava.
5. This red circle is actually a fruit! It's used as a sauce on pizza and pasta.

Down

1. An orange root vegetable that rabbits like to eat.
2. A red root vegetable that sounds a bit like what you do with vegetables: you eat them!
3. These little green seeds grow together in a pod.
4. These starchy root vegetables can be mashed, roasted, hashed, or fried into french fries.

Bodies of Water

STREAM   POND   LAKE   RIVER   OCEAN   FLOAT

NSTRUCTIONS: Solve the clues to fill in the puzzle.

Across

1. Smaller than a lake, this body of water is a natural pool. Ducks or fish might live in it.
4. Bigger than a pond, this body of water is surrounded by land on all sides
5. A small river, also called a creek or a brook.

Down

2. Like the Atlantic or Pacific, this body of water is huge and salty! It surrounds entire continents.
3. Things that are light will __ on top of the water, which is how things move downstream.

6. Bigger than a stream, this body of water is long and moves fast; it might lead to the ocean.

In the Kitchen

POTS   FRIDGE   STOVE   OVEN   FREEZER   BOARD

INSTRUCTIONS: Solve the clues to fill in the puzzle.

Across

2. The __ keeps food ice cold.
5. A __top is where you cook food in a pan.

Down

1. To bake something, you put it in the __.
2. A __, short for refrigerator, keeps food cool.
3. You probably have __ and pans in your kitchen to cook with.
4. People can use knives to chop things up on a piece of wood called a cutting __.

Outer Space

SUN   MOON   MARS   SHOOT   EARTH   SPACE

INSTRUCTIONS: Solve the clues to fill in the puzzle.

Across

1. The red planet.
3. All the planets are out in __.
4. The bright circular object we see in the sky at night.
5. The planet we live on.

Down

2. When you wish upon a __ing star, you're actually seeing a meteor as rock burns up in Earth's atmosphere.
3. The big star we see during the day, which is also the center of our solar system.

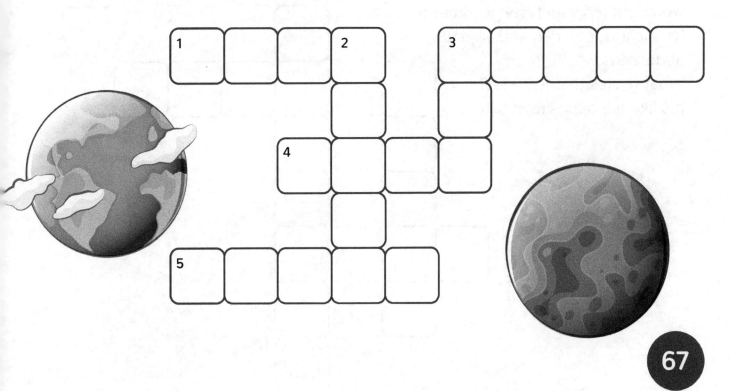

Sweet Treats

CHOCOLATE   SUGAR   CAKE   CARA   COOKIE   PIE

INSTRUCTIONS: Solve the clues to fill in the puzzle.

Across

2. A small, round baked good with flavors like chocolate chip or snickerdoodle.
4. You might eat this to celebrate your birthday.
5. If you melt sugar, you can make __mel syrup, which some people like to dip apples into.

Down

1. A crust with fruit or cream inside, with flavors like apple and pumpkin.
2. Also called "cocoa", this is a long word, but it's very tasty: it comes in bars, chips, powder, and all kinds of desserts.
3. What makes things sweet? It's like the opposite of salt.

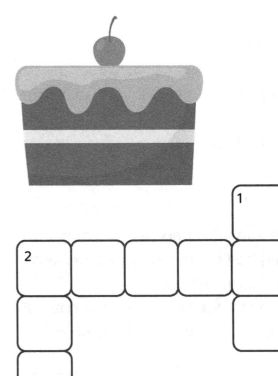

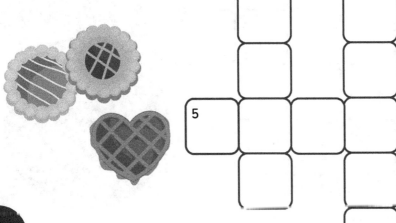

How Do You Feel?

ANGRY   HUNGRY   SAD   FUNNY   THIRSTY   TIRED

INSTRUCTIONS: Say how you feel to fill in the puzzle.

Across

2. When I don't sleep, I feel:
4. When I get mad, I feel:
5. When I tell you a joke and you laugh,
   I feel:

Down

1. When I cry, I feel:
2. When I need to drink water, I feel:
3. When I want food, I feel:

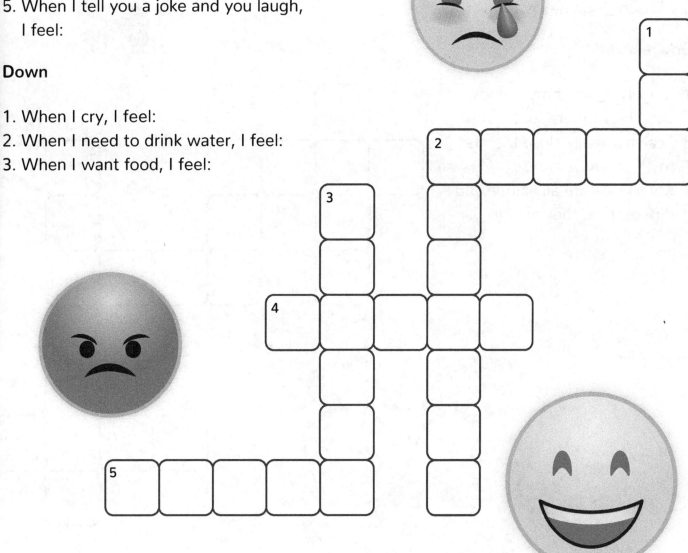

Me and My Friends

PLAY   TIME   SPECIAL   LIKE   NICE   BEST

INSTRUCTIONS: Talk about your friends to fill in the puzzle.

Across

3. My friends aren't mean, they are __.
5. I like to spend __ with my friends.
6. I like to __ games with my friends.

Down

1. I really __ all of my friends. And I love them too!
2. I call my really close friends my __ friends.
4. My friends are all unique and different, so they are all __.

What Is It Like?

SMELL   LOOK   TOUCH   SEE   HEAR   TASTE

NSTRUCTIONS: Solve the clues to fill in the puzzle.

Across

2. Use your ears to __ what something sounds like.
3. Use your eyes to __ something.
5. If you use your eyes, you'll know what things __ like.

Down

1. Use your tongue to __ something.
3. Use your nose to __ something.
4. Use your hands to __ something, and you'll find out how it feels.

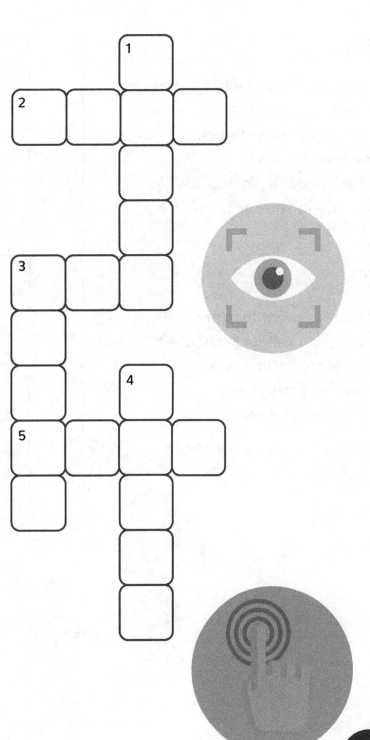

Let's Ask Questions

WHERE   WHAT   WHEN   WHO   WHICH   HOW

INSTRUCTIONS: Solve the clues to fill in the puzzle.

Across

1. If you don't know what something is, ask: "__ is this?"
2. You might ask someone: "__ are you doing today?"
4. To ask about a place or look for something you can't find, ask __ something is.

Down

1. If there is more than one option, ask "__ one should I choose?"
3. To ask about time, ask __ something happened.
4. To ask about a person, ask __.

This Sounds Like...

ATE   RIGHT   EIGHT   WRITE   WEAK   WEEK

INSTRUCTIONS: Figure out the homophones to fill in the puzzle.

Across

2. The opposite of strong. (Sounds like word #1.)
5. This number comes after seven. (Sounds like word #3.)

Down

1. Seven days, from Monday to Sunday.
   (Sounds like word #2 across.)
2. You can use a pen or pencil to __ words down.
   (Sounds like word #4.)
3. If you had a meal yesterday, you __ some food.
   (Sounds like word #5.)
4. The opposite of wrong. (Sounds like word #2 down.)

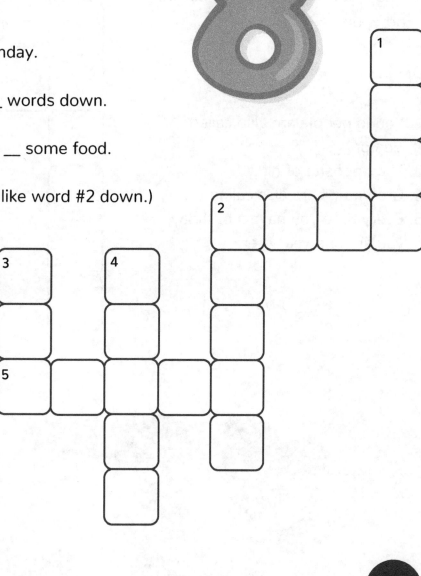

73

When You Grow Up

YOUNG   ADULTS   OLD   TALL   LEARN   CHILDREN

INSTRUCTIONS: Solve the clues to fill in the puzzle.

Across

3. As you grow up, you'll __ new things, like you __ new things in school.
6. You'll get bigger and __er as you grow up.

Down

1. Young people are also called kids or __.
2. The opposite of old.
4. Grown-ups are also called __.
5. Every time you have a birthday, you are one year __er.

74

So Many Things to Be!

WORK   MAIL   CHEF   FARMER   DRIVER   DENTIST

INSTRUCTIONS: Name the job to fill in the puzzle.

Across

2. A person who fixes teeth is called a:
5. A person who grows food and raises animals
   is called a:

Down

1. A person who delivers letters and packages is called a __ carrier.
2. A person who steers a bus is called a bus __.
3. A person who cooks food is called a:
4. People __ hard at all kinds of different jobs!

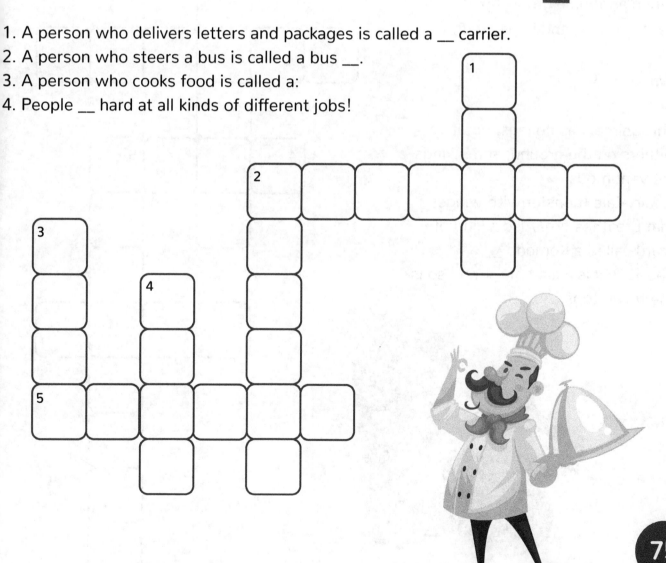

Reptiles and Amphibians

SCALES   TOAD   DINOSAUR   SNAKE   FROG   DRAGON

INSTRUCTIONS: Solve the clues to fill in the puzzle.

Across

3. Like fish, some reptiles have __ on their skin.
4. A frog can also be called a __, which is why mushrooms are sometimes called toadstools.
6. When a tadpole grows up, it becomes a __ and hops around.

Down

1. This animal has no legs, but it slithers on the ground; some kinds are venomous.
2. A fairy-tale monster with wings that breathes fire. Also a kind of lizard called a Komodo __.
5. The T. Rex is a kind of __, and so is the triceratops.

Something to Drink

LEMON   COFFEE   CUP   SHAKE   JUICE   SPILL

NSTRUCTIONS: Solve the clues to fill in the puzzle.

Across

1. If you tip your cup over, the drink will __ out.
4. This drink is made from fruits like apples and oranges.
5. This bitter drink is mostly for grown-ups; it has caffeine in it and makes them less tired.

Down

1. A milk__ is blended ice cream.
2. What do you put drinks inside of?
3. Juice made from a sour citrus fruit might be __ade

Let's Go Shopping

SALE   FOOD   SHOP   PET   STORE   MONEY

INSTRUCTIONS: Solve the clues to fill in the puzzle.

Across

3. A place where you go to buy things.
4. The things in a store are for __, but something might also be on __ if it costs less than usual.
5. You can buy __ to eat at the grocery store.

Down

1. Something you spend when you buy things; it can be coins or bills.
2. You can buy animals like dogs and cats at the __ store.
4. When you buy things at the store, it is called __ping.

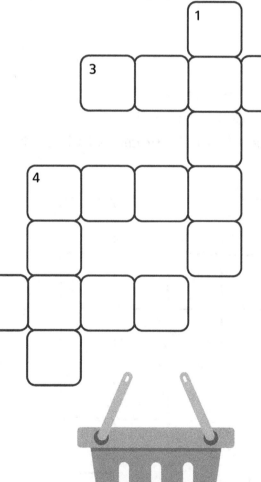

Level 3

That was awesome!
You're getting even better at this.

Since you're ready for something a little harder, each of these crossword puzzles has 7 or 8 clues to solve.

My Dog

WAG   STICK   WOOF   PAW   BARK   SIT   FETCH

INSTRUCTIONS: Solve the clues to fill in the puzzle.

Across

2. When big dogs bark, the sound they make is:
4. You can teach a dog to __ or lie down.
6. Cats meow, dogs __. This is also the word for the outside of a tree.

Down

1. A dog's foot is called a __.
3. You can play __ with your dog by throwing a ball for it to bring back.
4. A dog will chase a ball or a __, a small branch from a tree.
5. A happy dog will __ its tail.

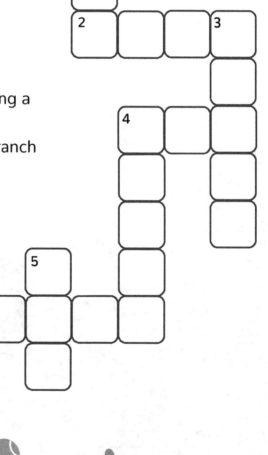

Volcanology

ERUPT   ASH   MAGMA   PEAK   LAVA   ROCKS   VOLCANO

INSTRUCTIONS: Solve the clues to fill in the puzzle.

Across

1. When magma flows out of a volcano,
   it is called __.
4. When lava is still inside the Earth before
   eruption, it is called __.
6. When a volcano explodes, it is called an __ion.
7. Lava is made of melted __ from inside the Earth.

Down

2. A __ is a break in the Earth's crust where lava
   can come out.
3. Some volcanoes are shaped like mountains.
   The very top of a mountain is called the:
5. When a volcano erupts, it shoots out bits of
   lava, rock, and __.

Let's Look for Treasure

HUNT   CHEST   MAP   GOLD   MONEY   HOLE   SHOVEL

INSTRUCTIONS: Solve the clues to fill in the puzzle.

Across

1. Follow a treasure __ to where the 'X' marks the spot.
2. Use a __ to dig for treasure.
4. Open up the treasure __ to see what's inside.
6. Treasures can be made of metal like silver and __.

Down

1. Some treasures are worth lots of __, so they're very valuable.
3. When you look for treasure, it's called a treasure __.
5. Dig a __ to find buried treasure.

In the Garden

GARDENER   GLOVES   HAT   PETALS   WORM   GRASS   DIRT

INSTRUCTIONS: Solve the clues to fill in the puzzle.

Across

4. A person who paints is a painter,
   a person who works in a garden is a __.
5. Wear a __ on your head to shade
   your eyes.
7. Wear __ to keep your hands clean.

Down

1. The earth, ground, or soil is also
   called __, it will make your hands __y.
2. Flowers like roses have lots of
   colorful __ that bloom out of buds.
3. This green plant grows everywhere,
   like all over your lawn.
6. This squiggly pink animal lives in
   the dirt.

Comic Book

INSTRUCTIONS: Solve the clues to fill in the puzzle.

Across

5. A hero with incredible powers is called a __.
6. Comics that make you laugh are __, so newspaper comics are called __ papers.

Down

1. Sunday comic strips are printed in the news__.
2. A short comic that appears in the newspaper is a comic __.
3. A superhero who can go fast has super __.
4. Comics can be put together in a comic __ that tells a story.
5. Heroes who are super __ can stop trains and lift up heavy cars.

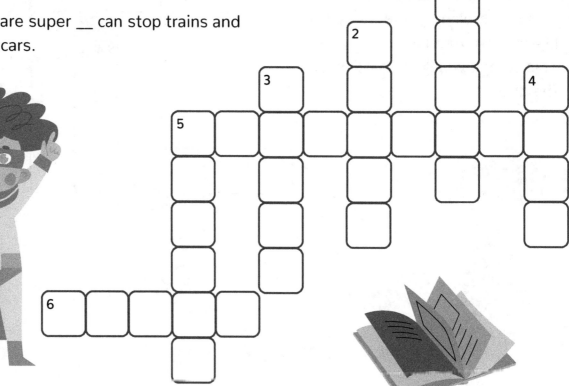

Let's Paint

PERSON   ARTIST   BLEND   SELF   BRUSH   PAINTING   HANG

INSTRUCTIONS: Solve the clues to fill in the puzzle.

Across

2. When you finish a painting, you can __ it up on the wall.
5. Painters use a special stick to paint, called a paint__.
7. Painters can mix or __ different colors together to make new ones.

Down

1. A painter uses paints to paint a __.
3. A painter makes art, so they are an __.
4. A portrait is a painting of a __.
6. A __-portrait is a painting the artist does of themselves.

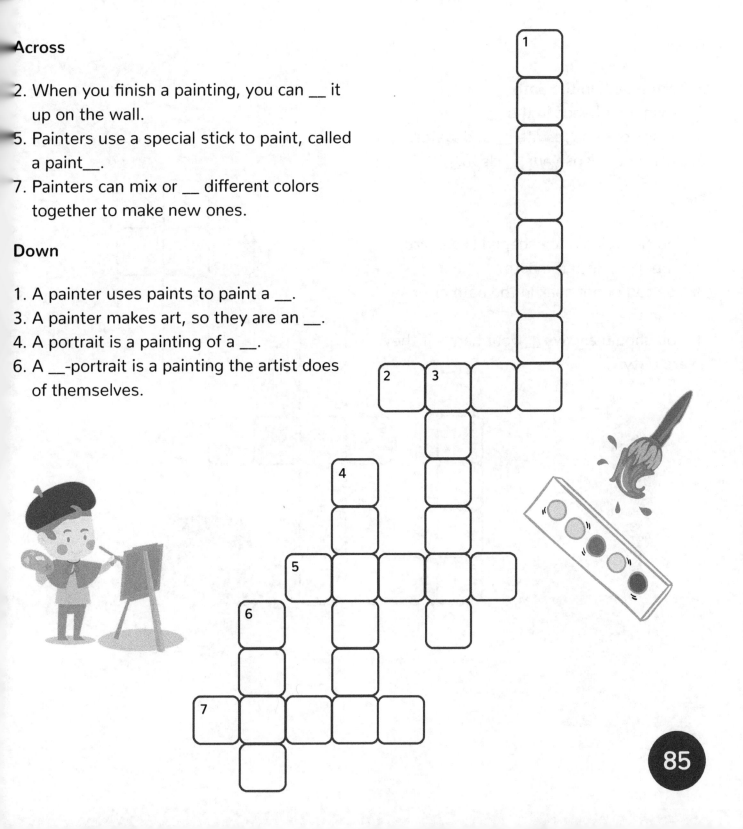

Bath Time

INSTRUCTIONS: Solve the clues to fill in the puzzle.

Across

2. Take a bath in the bath__.
3. Wash your hands in the __.
5. Wash your hands with __ and water.
6. Shampoo keeps your __ clean.

Down

1. You can bring a toy shaped like a bird, a rubber __, into the bath.
3. You can either soak in the bath or rinse off in the __.
4. You should always __ your hands if they are dirty.

Let's Play an Instrument !

INSTRUMENT   MARACA   SING   GUITAR   DRUM   SONG

INSTRUCTIONS: Solve the clues to fill in the puzzle.

Across

5. Anything you can make music with, including your voice, is an ___.

Down

1. Use your hands or __sticks on a __ to make a beat.
2. This instrument has six strings you can strum; they can be electric or acoustic.
3. A __ is a hollow instrument that rattles when you move it around.
4. Use your voice to __.
6. You can sing or play a __.

Let's Go Hiking

SOCKS   STICK   PACK   LOST   BOTTLE   SCREEN   TRAILS

INSTRUCTIONS: Solve the clues to fill in the puzzle.

Across

2. Remember to carry a __ of water with you.
4. You can carry things in your back__ when you hike.
6. Some people use a branch or cane as a walking __.
7. Bring a map or follow trail signs so you don't get __ in the woods.

Down

1. If it's sunny out, wear sun__ so you don't get burned.
3. The paths you hike on are called __.
5. Under your hiking shoes, you might wear a thick pair of __.

Lunch in the Park

BREAD   BLANKET   BASKET   PICNIC   SIDE   FRUIT   FRESH

INSTRUCTIONS: Solve the clues to fill in the puzzle.

Across

1. Baked food that comes in buns or loaves.
2. For a picnic, you can pack food into a __.
4. The opposite of inside is out__.
5. Apples, oranges, peaches, or pears are all kinds of __.

Down

1. Bring a towel or __ to sit on.
3. When you eat outside, it is called a __.
5. Outside, you can enjoy the __ air.

In My Family

INSTRUCTIONS: Solve the clues to fill in the puzzle.

Across

1. A parent who is a man.
6. A parent who is a woman.
7. A sibling who is a girl.
8. Your parent's brother.

Down

2. Your parent's sister.
3. A sibling who is a boy.
4. A sibling who is older than you can be called this, the opposite of "little".
5. Your parents' parents are your __parents, like __ma and __pa.

90

Let's Go Camping

GROUND   COMPASS   TENT   BAG   HOTDOG   CAMP   FLASH   FISHING

INSTRUCTIONS: Solve the clues to fill in the puzzle.

Across

1. Bring a __light to light your path at night.
3. A __ will point the way so you don't get lost.
4. When you camp, you sleep in a canvas house called a __.
5. The place you set up your tent is a campsite or camp__; this is also what you sleep on when you camp!
6. You can stay warm at night in your sleeping __.

Down

1. If you bring a rod, reel, and hook, you can go __ in the river.
2. You can roast this sausage on a stick; eat it with ketchup and a bun...
3. Bring wood to light a __fire.

Shooting Hoops

PLAYER   POINT   PASS   HOOP   SHOOT   BASKET   NET   FOUL

INSTRUCTIONS: Solve the clues to fill in the puzzle.

Across

3. If a player hurts another player or does something wrong, it's called a __.
   This word also means "bad".

4. This game with a hoop, net, ball, and court is called __ball.

6. The circle you want a basketball to go into is called the:

8. The thing hanging from the hoop is a mesh __, you might also use one of these to catch things.

Down

1. A player wins at least one __ any time they score without making a foul and can get as many as three with one shot.

2. Everyone who plays in a game is a __.

5. When players __, they throw the ball at the hoop to try and score.

7. When players throw the ball to each other, it is called a __.

In the Bakery

HEAT   FLOUR   BAKER   BUNS   APRON   BAKE   BAKERY   LOAF

INSTRUCTIONS: Solve the clues to fill in the puzzle.

Across

3. Bread is sold at this store.
5. Some bread is made with white wheat powder called __.
6. Little round balls of bread.
7. The __ of the oven will bake things.

Down

1. A person who bakes.
2. One big piece of bread that can be sliced into pieces.
4. Wear an __ in the kitchen to keep your clothes clean.
6. What you do to dough to make it into bread.

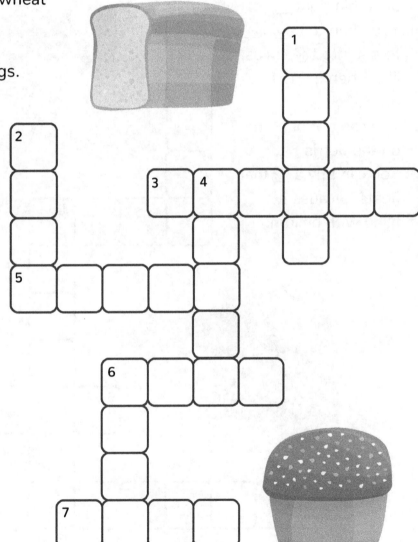

Circus Tent

EATER   WHEEL   BACK   TAMER   TICKET   ROPE   ELEPHANT   BALLOON

INSTRUCTIONS: Solve the clues to fill in the puzzle.

Across

2. Some acrobats walk high above the crowd on a thin tight__.
4. You need to buy a __ to get into the circus, like when going to a movie.
5. You can go for a ride on the Ferris __.
6. You can buy a __ that floats because it's filled with helium.

Down

1. A performer who can put fire in their mouth is called a fire__, but don't try to eat fire at home!
3. This is a huge animal with a trunk and tusks.
4. A person who can control lions is a lion __.
6. Some people are trick riders; they ride on the __of a horse and do stunts.

CIRCUS TICKET

CIRCUS TICKET

Ballet Dancer

GRACE   CIRCLE   PRETTY   MEN   KNEE   BALLERINAS   BALLET   LEAP

INSTRUCTIONS: Solve the clues to fill in the puzzle.

Across

2. Women who dance ballet.
4. Ballerinas can __ or jump through the air.
6. Ballet is a beautiful dance; things that are beautiful are also:
8. To "plie", ballerinas bend their legs at the __ joint.

Down

1. When a ballerina pirouettes, she spins in a __.
3. A graceful kind of dance that uses pointe shoes.
5. Ballerinas are very __ful; the opposite of clumsy.
7. __ who dance ballet can be called "ballerinos".

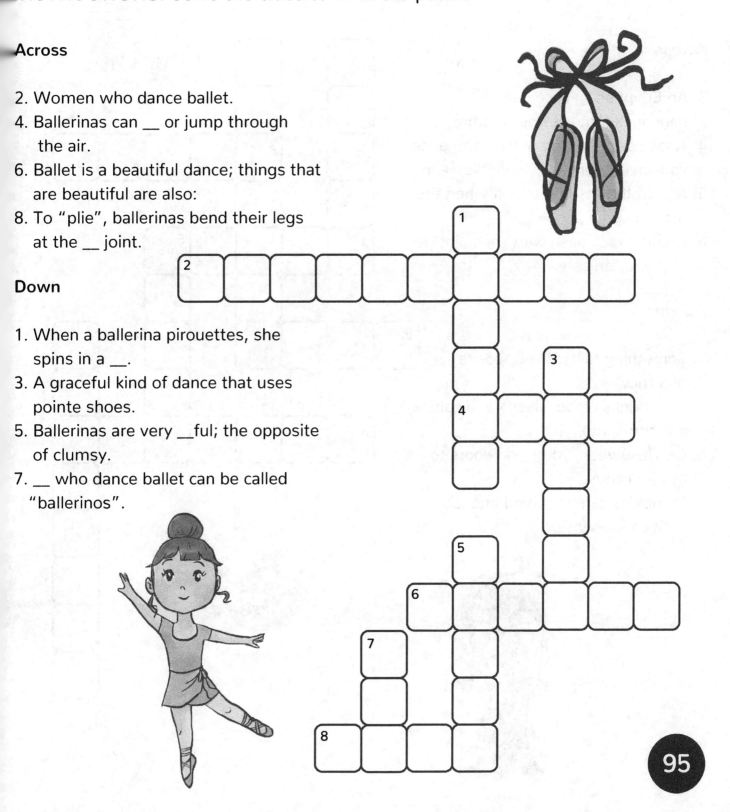

It's Halloween!

INSTRUCTIONS: Solve the clues to fill in the puzzle.

Across

3. An Egyptian __ is covered in bandages (not like your mommy).
4. A joke or prank you pull on someone; you say "__ or treat" on Halloween.
6. A __wolf turns into a wolf when the moon is full.
8. An orange squash with seeds inside that you can carve.

Down

1. Something tasty, the opposite of a trick.
2. A __ drinks blood, sleeps in a coffin, and turns into a bat.
5. On Halloween, you __ on doors to ask for candy.
7. Pumpkins can be carved into jack'o'__ with candles inside.

96

Play Ball

BASEBALL   BASES   HOME   FIELD   MASCOTS   GLOVE   STRIKE   BAT

INSTRUCTIONS: Solve the clues to fill in the puzzle.

Across

2. When a ball is hit out of the field, it is a __run.
4. This game with bats and balls is called __.
6. Catch the ball with a mitt or baseball __.
7. If your bat misses the ball, it's called a __. Three of these means you're out!

Down

1. Play on a baseball __ shaped like a diamond.
3. Some teams have __, animals or people who represent the team.
4. The field has three __ and a home plate, which is why the sport is called baseball.
5. Use a stick called a __ to hit the baseball.

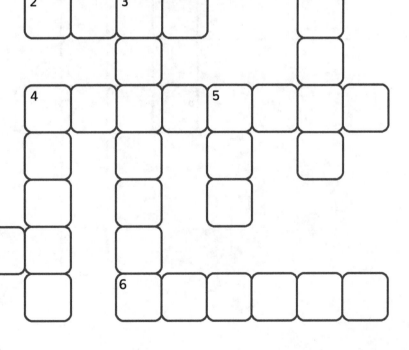

It's Winter

INSTRUCTIONS: Solve the clues to fill in the puzzle.

Across

2. Go ice __ on a frozen lake.
3. Frozen water.
4. Start a fire in the fire__.
6. Make snow into these circles to throw them.

Down

1. These knit gloves will keep your hands warm.
3. A sharp piece of ice that hangs off a roof.
5. Ponds are usually __ into ice in the Winter because they get so cold.
7. A frozen man.

A Trip to Hawaii

PINE   LACE   SURF   AIRPLANE   ISLANDS   STRINGS   PALM   RAINBOWS

INSTRUCTIONS: Solve the clues to fill in the puzzle.

Across

4. You have to take a boat or fly on an __ to get to Hawaii.
7. Maui, Kauai, Hawaii, and Honolulu are all small __ in the ocean.

Down

1. The lei is a strand of flowers you wear around your neck like a neck__.
2. The __apple is a spiky tropical fruit.
3. Because it rains so often in Hawaii, there are many colorful __.
5. Coconuts grow on __ trees.
6. A ukulele is like a small guitar, but it has four __ to strum instead of six.
8. In Hawaii, people use __boards to __ on the ocean waves.

Bonus Level

Wow, you got through all of that, and you're still ready to solve more puzzles? We've got something special for you!

These crosswords are extra hard, and each of them has 9 or 10 words to figure out from the clues. We believe in you!

Fly Like a Bird

TELE   BIRD   FEATHER   GULL   HUMMING   BEAK   WOOD   NEST   OWL

INSTRUCTIONS: Solve the clues to fill in the puzzle.

Across

1. A __pecker is a bird that pecks holes in trees.
4. A sea__ is a white bird that lives by the beach.
7. Birds might rest up on a __phone wire.
8. A bird lives in a __ made of sticks.
9. A black__ and a blue__ are both a type of flying animal.

Down

2. This bird says 'hoot hoot' and stays awake all night.
3. A __bird is a small bird that drinks flower nectar and flies very fast.
5. If you find a pretty __, it probably fell off a bird's wing.
6. A bird eats with its __.

Explore the World

GLOBE   TRIP   STATES   AIR   SUB   CASE   EGYPT   TOWER   GREAT

INSTRUCTIONS: Solve the clues to fill in the puzzle.

Across

1. In France, you can see the Eiffel __.
2. The great pyramids are in __, with the Sphinx.
5. Explore the ocean in a __marine.
6. The __ Wall of China is more than 13,000 miles long.
7. Pack everything into your suit__.

Down

1. When you go on vacation, you take a __ somewhere.
3. The map of the world can spin on a __.
4. You can fly through the sky in a hot __ balloon or on an __plane.
5. There are fifty __ in the USA (United __ of America).

At the Pizzeria

RONI   CRUST   SHARE   LARGE   CHEESE   TOMATO   CUT   BOX   PIZZA

INSTRUCTIONS: Solve the clues to fill in the puzzle.

Across

2. Peppe__ is a popular pizza topping.
3. Pizza usually has white mozzarella __ on it.
5. What is the bread part of a pizza called?
7. What food does a pizzeria serve?
8. Pizza comes in a cardboard __.

Down

1. You can buy a small, medium, or __ pizza.
3. __ a pizza into slices to eat it.
4. You can __ pizza slices with all your friends.
6. You can make a __ into red pizza sauce.

Mythical Creatures

HUMAN   MAID   MAGICAL   LIFE   MONSTER   ZOMBIE
UNICORN   ALIENS   FOOT   LUCK

INSTRUCTIONS: Solve the clues to fill in the puzzle.

Across

2. These creatures live on other planets.
4. A creature that crawls out of graveyards and wants brains.
6. A mer__ is half human and half fish.
9. A horse with one beautiful horn.

Down

1. A centaur is half horse and half __.
3. A phoenix burns up into ash and then comes back to __.
5. Creatures that can do magic are __ creatures.
6. The Loch Ness __ is also called Nessie.
7. Leprechauns bring good __.
8. This huge, ape-like creature is called big__ because of the huge prints it leaves.

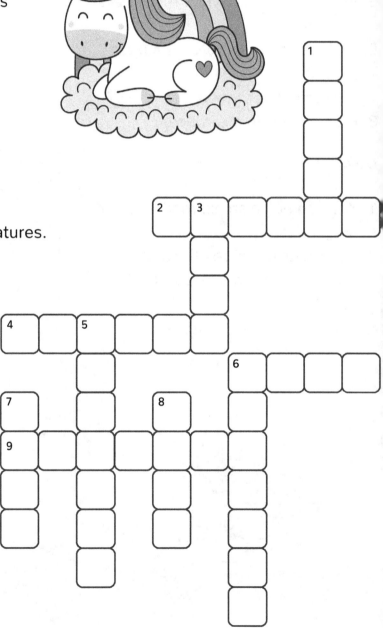

This, Not That

INSTRUCTIONS: Solve the clues to fill in the puzzle.

Across

2. The opposite of expensive.
6. The opposite of weird.
7. The opposite of hard or firm.
8. The opposite of long.
9. The opposite of good.

Down

1. The opposite of closed.
3. The opposite of full.
4. The opposite of rough.
5. The opposite of quiet.
8. The opposite of fast.

105

The Places You'll Go

PLAYGROUND   CIRCUS   GARDEN   BEACH   MUSEUM   FARM
ZOO   LIBRARY   STORE   HOSPITAL

INSTRUCTIONS: Solve the clues to fill in the puzzle.

Across

4. A place where you grow plants.
6. A place where art and history are on display.
8. A place where people go to see a doctor when they're sick.
10. A place where lots of animals, like lions and tigers, are on display for you to visit.

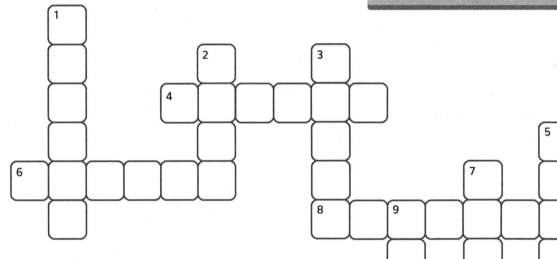

Down

1. A place where clowns, acrobats, and trick-riders perform.
2. A place where food is grown and animals are raised.
3. A place where the ocean meets the land; you can see sand, boats, and waves.
5. A place where you can play with your friends, like on a jungle gym.
7. A place where you can read and check out books.
9. A place where you go shopping and buy things.

CONGRATULATIONS!

You're truly amazing! Even though it got pretty hard, you persisted and finished all of the puzzles. What a fantastic job!

If you want to continue with some more crosswords, just send me an email at hello.jennifer.trace@gmail.com, and I'll send you back some printable puzzles to fill out for free.

My name is Jennifer Trace, and I hope you found this workbook helpful and fun. If you have any suggestions for how to improve this book, please let me know through the email above.

If you liked this book, please leave me a positive review on Amazon.

Thank you very much!

Jennifer Trace

Congratulations
Crossword Puzzle Star:

THE BEST!

_____

Date:_____   Signed:_____

CPSIA information can be obtained
at www.ICGtesting.com
Printed in the USA
LVHW100954301120
673007LV00004B/5